Parabellum

A Performer's Guide To Hecklers

By
Wayne Goodman

Parabellum

Copyright © 2020 Wayne Goodman Entertainments.
All rights reserved

No part of this book shall be reproduced or transmitted in any form or by any means, electronic or mechanical, including photocopying, recording, or by any information retrieval system without written permission of the author.

Published by Wayne Goodman Entertainments.
For more copies of this book please email:
wayne@waynegoodman.co.uk
Tel: (+44) 07726 190078
Designed and Set by Wayne Goodman Entertainments

ISBN 978-0-9928201-4-5

www.waynegoodman.co.uk

Edited by Johnny Toro

Although every precaution has been taken in the preparation of this book, the publisher and author assume no responsibility for errors or omissions. Neither is any liability assumed for damages resulting from the use of this information contained herein.

CAN'T AFFORD THIS BOOK?
A percentage of every book sold subsidises another for those who cannot afford a copy.

If you genuinely cannot afford this book & would like to apply for a subsidised copy please contact wayne@waynegoodman.co.uk

"Dear heckler, from my fear of you, I have learned to love you" Wayne Goodman

This book is dedicated to my beautiful daughter
Charlee Goodman
I love you to the moon and back and twice around the universe.

This book would not have been possible without the help of:

My Mum for supporting me all these years through thick and thin.

Special thanks to Deborah Murray and Family

Oliver Smith
Christian Fletcher
Mike Rose
Peter Nardi
Dave Loosley
Stacy Smith and Rebecca Bryan
The Members of the Ipswich Magical Society

Special Thanks to Simon Shaw & Frankie Shaw for more support than I can ever thank you for

Special thanks to three men who continue to inspire, amaze and who have shown true friendship.

Brian Watson
Michael Murray
Jasper Blakeley

Contents

Foreword	6
Introduction	9
Why do people heckle	12
You have been heckled	15
Types of heckler	19
The different types of heckle	22
Performer response styles	26
Friendly fire	29
Enemy fire	33
The double decker	34
The group	37
The microphone grabber	41
When venue staff attack	43
The act assassin	45
Damien	50
Body language	55
Controlling the banter	57
Responding	59
Using heckle lines	61
Heckle lines	66
Not using heckle lines	71

They carry on heckling	73
They still carry on heckling using heckle lines	80
They still carry on heckling not using heckle lines	82
Crossing the line	85
Using to the heckler	88
The three strike rule	91
Things you can use against the heckler	95
Using the audience	97
The close up magician	103
Conclusion	105
Notes	108
Also by Wayne Goodman	109

Foreword

When Wayne asked me to write the foreword to this book on heckling I didn't hesitate in saying yes, not just because Wayne is such a lovely bloke, but because dealing with hecklers has been such a large part of my own performing life.

To be honest I personally wouldn't have known where to start writing a book like this since I'd always felt I'd dealt with hecklers instinctively, however having read this book, I now know my instincts were in fact entirely fashioned through experience.

As performers we can often forget where we started, how bad we were in the beginning at controlling situations and reading rooms. I've been lucky enough to perform as a headline stand-up comic for several years in some of the best comedy clubs across the UK as my Russian alter ego, 'Kockov', and getting to this point has partly been my ability to deal with hecklers.

However (and I'm sure Wayne will agree) the fact that I'd spent five years working as a children's entertainer throughout south Wales and The Valleys gave me the tools necessary to control children, after that adults were a breeze.

Performing as a larger-than-life character in comedy clubs and always coming on last, mostly to up to four hundred alcohol-fuelled stag, hen and work mates, until reading this book I'd never stopped to analyse what was being shouted at me and by whom.

It turns out I am "The Joker" (in the chapter 'Performer Response Styles') "The Joker" Hits back with line after line, will pick up anything happening in the room and use that against the heckler.

The Joker does not believe in compromise, he will deal with the heckler and get back on with the show without stopping for breath. The "Joker" will have a joke or line for every situation, heckle or not and will defeat any heckler without breaking a sweat.

I hadn't realised what I did had a name, but then again to really think that what you do is 'unique', is foolish.

I've always been fearful of over-analysing how I get laughs in case it turns out I'm "all fur coat and no knickers" – essentially looking behind the curtain to see just an old man pulling levers.

I've always believed in constantly educating myself and learning new skills, but if I'm totally honest, I didn't think I was going to learn anything new from reading this book, I was wrong.

Wayne is an obsessive, he has an encyclopaedic mind when it comes to lines and jokes and I'm yet to meet someone who knows more about American stand-ups. Couple this vast knowledge with Wayne's years of experience having performed in every conceivable scenario and you have to take what he's written within these pages seriously.

Only after reading this book do I now realise how I could have handled several hecklers better, especially the women.

If I'd only known Wayne's brilliant insight into dealing with abusive drunk female hecklers, maybe I'd have had several better gigs.

I've seen professional hecklers destroy decent comics on stage all because the comic wasn't equipped to deal with it, yes, nothing can ever replace experience, but this book can certainly go a long way in preparing ANY performer to take command and control of any stage, any situation and anything that gets shouted at them.

I'll leave you with this final thought. Without naming names, (but let's say they're a current arena-filling UK stand-up comic and one of the biggest names in comedy on television) and a couple of years ago this big comic was doing a small comedy club gig trying out new material for an already sold out national stadium tour, and it didn't go well.

In the one hundred strong crowd was a man and woman who were professional hecklers, and the several acts on earlier in the evening had dealt with them very well and the room had accepted the banter thrown at the comics as they came on stage.

Unfortunately this big name comic wasn't interested in engaging them, instead he 'lost it' and ended up walking off stage in a huff after less than ten minutes. The moral of this story is, maybe if this book was available then and he'd read it, he'd have kept it together and things would have turned out differently. No matter how big a name you are, you're only as good as your last gig.

So please read this book and suggest it as vital reading to anyone who ever intends to step out onto a stage, it might just save their act.

Jasper Blakeley aka Kockov

Introduction

I started forming this book in my head and on little notes in a book back in 1996 whilst working as a magician on the ships. This sounds glamorous but it was "North Sea Ferries", the working men's clubs of the sea.

The actual work of turning it into a book did not start until the winter of 2002. I was working in Spain and wanted to start putting pen to paper. The main bulk of the book was written over the next few years, but due to life getting in the way, the book has been shelved again and again.

In 2006 the very funny comedy magician Keith Fields published his book "*How to handle hecklers*" which was an updated and enhanced version of his addition to the brilliant "*The magic of show business for the 1990's*" by Simon Lovell.

Both these books are excellent and well worth a read and a place in any magical library.

In 2014 I wrote and published "The definitive guide to restaurant magic". In 2016 I updated and released the book under it's new name of "The Expert at the Restaurant Table.

After publishing that book I decided it was time to finish this book.

Everyone gets heckled. Some more than others, some encourage it, some do not, however it is how you deal with it that defines your performance.

You need to be prepared for what you are facing. I do not want this book to be all doom and gloom, but it is important to know what can happen and be prepared for the consequences of your choices.

I wanted to make sure that this book would be different from others on the same subject, and have included ideas, concepts and thoughts which I've never seen in print before.

Unless otherwise stated the hecklers in this book will be referred to as male.

There is one word that appears in this book more than any other.

Control

It is by far the most important factor in any performance.
You have to learn how to control:
- Your nerves
- Your audience
- Your misdirection
- Any hecklers
- Your volunteers
- The surroundings
- The running of the show
- The atmosphere of the room

You are in charge and everyone knows that.
If the ceiling falls in and the room explodes everyone will look to you for instructions on what to do next.

An example of this kind of control is evident when you finish your routine, look up and say, "*Thank you*", and the audience bursts into applause, they are waiting for your cue.

So from this how do you control the heckler?
How do you make them do exactly what you want?

Well it's not that simple, otherwise you could just get the heckler to be quiet.

However by using the techniques described in this book you will have a better understanding of the ways to control the situation.

It is only through years of performing that I have learned the fundamentals of what it takes to handle the situations that arise when on stage.

A master storyteller holds the audience spellbound, completely under their control.

They nod when he wants, they laugh, cry, clap and cheer exactly when the performer desires.

This works for every aspect of the show, including hecklers. You make the decisions on how to work the heckler, use lines, don't use lines, hit them hard or hit them soft.

It all comes down to control. Your control!

This book is aimed as a reference tool, some performers will go forever without being heckled, some like me, get heckled at almost every gig.

Use it to enhance your performance, add it to the tools you use, and keep ready for when you may need it.

I hope you enjoy reading this book and thank you for your continued support.

Wayne Goodman

Chapter One
Why Do People Heckle?

The all important question, "Why do people heckle?"
This is a hard question to answer.

Comedians and comedy acts get heckled, very rarely do other types of performers get this kind of interruption.

The reason for this is that as a comedy act or magic act you are interacting with the audience on a personal level.

You may ask questions or invite members of the audience on stage, something a singer, or a dance group would not be doing.

This means you are inviting the spectators to take an active part of the show and thus some people may believe that they have a right to say something.

There are many reasons why someone might heckle you.

Something you have said
You have said or done something that has stirred an emotion or opinion and they feel that they must say something.

This can be problematic if you have offended them, as they will be hard to quieten.

This is tricky and you may have a problem on your hands.
you need to act quickly and professionally.

You need to evaluate the situation quickly and act accordingly. If you have offended someone you will need to follow the advice in "Crossing the Line".

Remember this is just a response to something you have said, unless you can make use of it, then the best thing to do is just laugh it off or ignore it and move on.

Impressing someone.
They are trying to impress friends, a girl, a boy or friends in a group.

Never a nice situation as the more you beat them the more they will want to fight back, not unlike a bad gambler hunting that elusive big win, they need to keep betting just hoping that the next one is the one that they need.

This kind of heckler is not normally funny however and a few well chosen lines can keep him quiet without bruising his ego too much.

They are drunk.
Enough said. They have had too much to drink and now they think they are the entertainer.

The best course of action in this situation is to follow the advice regarding the "Drunk" in the chapter "If they carry on heckling".

They think they are funny or funnier than you.
They are going to be quite persistent and will try their amazingly funny wit on you.

If you do get a funny heckler then you should exploit the fact and use it to your advantage, and if they are not funny then following the advice regarding the "Would be or failed" should soon have your show back on track

They have something to contribute, whether you want it or not.
Some people are just plain rude. They don't have the ability to keep quiet and lack the social skills of normal people.

This is more annoying than anything else, but dealt with properly this is an easy heckler to put down. What you don't want to do is encourage them too much, as they may think they have a free pass to be part of your show.

They are a professional heckler.
They think that they are God, and they think they can beat or better you.

This is a dangerous and wild animal, and very hard to deal with.

I have seen seasoned professionals destroyed by this kind of heckler. We shall examine him more later and look at the best ways of dealing with him.

If you can determine the reason for the heckle, you can decide the right course of action.

If you are continually getting heckled show after show then it is obviously either the way you present your act or the type of audience you are performing for.

If this is the case, you must realise your options.

- Change your style or show to accommodate the hecklers.
- Change the type of shows you get booked for, i.e. look at your target audience.

There are some comedians who actually encourage hecklers, they use the interaction as the base of their act, however this is not for the inexperienced, it is a very dangerous way to perform.

I actually like a good heckle, as a comedy performer I can use the situation to my advantage, but I have confidence in my ability to control and direct the audience so as not to affect or lose the pace, tempo or quality of the show.

I would never attempt to compete with a heckler if I didn't feel like I had complete control over the room and the audience.

It's not worth trying to take on a heckler if it is a possibility that the audience will turn on you. You will need their support, more than anything else if you wish to carry on after the banter is over.

Chapter Two
You Have Been Heckled

You are partway through your show, and all of a sudden, someone in the audience shouts something out.

You have just been heckled.

The first reaction will be **Panic**.

Your mouth runs dry, you start to sweat, the room starts to spin and you look left and right to see if there is anyone to help you but there is not.

You look into the audience for what you can see, maybe a friendly face will help you back on track, but everyone is either laughing or looking at you, expectantly waiting for your response to the heckle.

A cold feeling runs down your back as you desperately try to think of something to say.

- What has just happened?
- How do you react?
- Is this the beginning of the end?

What has happened?
Someone, one person has decided that they want to be part of the show, and has vocally entered the fray.

How do you react?
This is a big question, there are a lot of different ways to react and in this book we are going to look at all of them.

To start with however, let's keep it simple and just say "do not panic". Keep calm, stay in control and evaluate what has happened.

Is this the beginning of the end?
Of course not. A lot of people automatically think that the heckler is against you, this is not always the case.

The heckle is a response from the audience, either to something you have said or done, it may not be malicious, it may get a laugh that actually adds to the show.

There are so many different routes to take at this point.

Before you choose which way to go you must look at the information available to you.

This process of choosing your next move and actually doing it must take microseconds to decide, too much of a pause and the audience will detect that you are hesitant and then they will move in for the kill.

So how do you make this decision?

How do you choose the correct course of action?

Where is the information that will point you in the correct direction?

Everything is against you. You have no time to think.

The pace of the show is at stake and everyone from the heckler who is preparing his next piece of infinite wisdom, to the audience who are waiting for a response to the heckler, to the man who pays your fee is looking at you waiting for you to carry on with your show.

So no pressure!

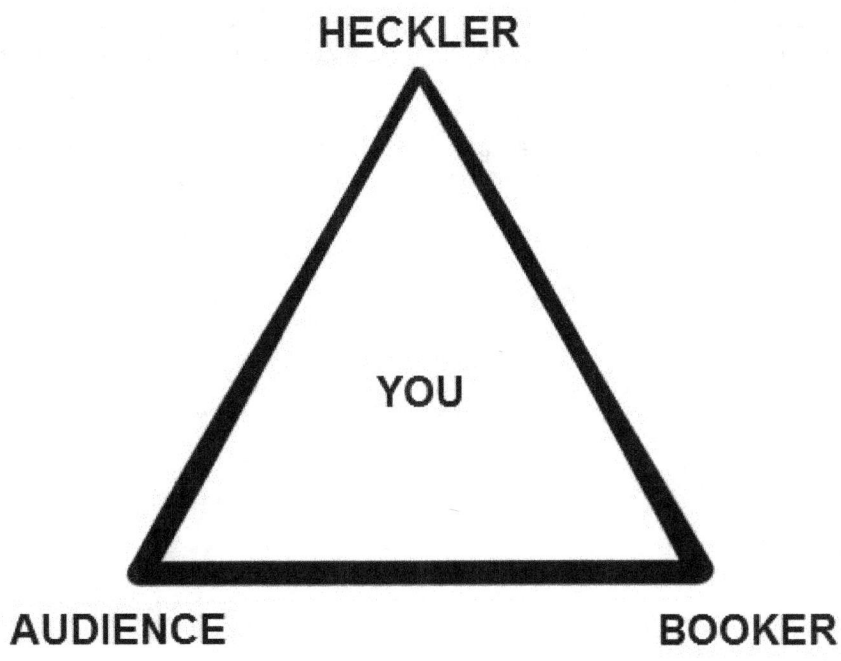

What should be happening in your head?

What should you be thinking at this point?

I was once told that a good performer is like a chess player. A good chess player is always thinking at least 5 or 6 moves ahead.

they have worked out every possible outcome from any possible move, nothing is discounted, even the most improbable of moves is calculated and possibilities examined.

You never know what the next move will be so you must be ready to change direction at any time.

After speaking to some great chess players I would alter this slightly to say that the greatest chess players think only one move ahead, but it is always the right move.

The first thing you need to learn is how to anticipate interruptions.

Watch how the audience is when you arrive, see how they react when you come on, if there is an act on before you then watch the reaction they get and so on.

You will learn to read these signs without even thinking about them, you will recognise signals and spot situations before they even happen.

Chapter Three
Types Of Heckler

There are a number of different types of hecklers.
Some will try to help and some to destroy, and you must learn how to differentiate between them.

To understand how to deal with the heckler, first we need to look at each type of heckler and their characteristics, we will look at how to deal with them later in the book.

Ladies and Gentleman
Please let me introduce The Hecklers.

The Comic.
This is a genuinely funny guy, he has a line or remark that gets a laugh.

The comic is not normally a disruption to the show and knows the concept of comedy. He knows that the whole basis of comedy is timing and he doesn't want to kill your act.

The only real problem he presents is when he gets excited and starts heckling more and more.

It can also encourage other people to have a go and heckle, which is an area you really want to avoid.

The Drunk.
Has had too much to drink and wants the dancing girls back on stage, doesn't want to watch you and your unequal ropes routine and will either shout abuse or random thoughts during your act.

He is very likely a microphone grabber and may even want to sing a song for the audience.

This is one of the most common hecklers and most of the time the person heckling is known for this behaviour. If dealt with correctly can be an easy adversary.

The Hardcore or Idiot.
Goes to comedy clubs a lot. He thinks he is funny, he will be the loud one in a group, he will want to be the centre of attention, the group comedian, he is the company funny guy, he laughs out loud at his own jokes, thinks he is invincible and isn't scared of you or your lines.

He thinks that he is a professional heckler but in reality he doesn't have any comedic timing or knowledge.

He won't like that you are funny and he wants his mates to see him upstage you.

You are nothing to him, he gets a massive boost to his ego and thinks it's really funny to ruin everyone else's fun.

This Heckler can be dangerous, very dangerous. If dealt with wrong he can also become part of "The Group".

The Would Be or Failed Comedian.
Wants to be the one on stage may be trying to help your act and sometimes (Very rarely) can be quite funny.

He has the ability to go over the top, and can encourage others to start heckling. He wants to help and really wants to contribute to the show and help move the act along.

Not really a worry if dealt with correctly.

The Group.
Can be one of two things, either they will want to make you or break you.

Not easy to deal with, but not impossible. You should be prepared to face an uphill battle against the group.

They will vary in shape, size and content, sometimes all male/female or sometimes mixed. "The Group" is a powerful enemy, but can be turned into a powerful friend with the right tactics.

The Female Heckler.
The most dangerous of all hecklers, has the ability to destroy you, with almost no chance of regrouping afterwards.

Must be dealt with correctly and very carefully. If you make a mistake here it could cost you more than just personal and professional pride.

You must keep the audience on side with you because the female heckler will use every dirty trick in the book, but you must remain professional.

I know this sounds really unfair and the bad news is, it is unfair, however it gives you the opportunity to remain in control and finish your show.

The Child Heckler.
The child heckler takes many forms, from annoying to drunk, they are not very dangerous if dealt with correctly however can be very dangerous if dealt with incorrectly.

The child heckler and the female are my least favourite hecklers and luckily they are few and far between, however they do occur and like all rare occurrences they are never quiet or un-noticed.

The Professional Heckler.
Another dangerous heckler is the professional. He is someone who regularly goes to comedy clubs, he probably heckles at the clubs and has knowledge of what can kill an act.

Unfortunately there are not many professional hecklers who want to help an act so we have to be ready for hard and harsh abuse from this heckler.

The professional will not be diverted by clever lines or subtle body language so you have to be ready to stand firm.

So there we have our eight favourite people, now we shall have a look at the different types of heckle.

Chapter Four
The Different Kinds of Heckle

There are many different types of heckle and here we will highlight the main ones that you will encounter.

The Abusive Heckle.
Not nice, usually from a "Hardcore" or "Drunk". These types of hecklers are becoming more common.

The abusive heckle will be aimed at your status or the quality of your act.

It will almost always contain some form of obscenity.

Remain professional at all times and use the fact that they have to use bad language to try and be funny.

The abusive heckle will normally be from a single person and will not reflect the opinion of the audience.

If on the other hand the whole audience agrees and starts to follow suit then an examination of your show or presentation is required.

The Funny Heckle.
Unfortunately these types of heckles are few and far between but they do happen, I will take it and use it. You can even remember it, a good heckle can be adapted and added permanently to your show. I will sometimes let the heckler have his moment,

I stop, I laugh, if it is a really funny heckle I may lose it (corpse) for a second and then congratulate the heckler with a "well done mate" or "good one" and carry on.

The only problem with the funny heckle is that the heckler may well try again, unless you are very lucky this second heckle will not be funny or as funny as the first.

Let them know you are in charge and carry on.

The Irrelevant Heckle.
These types of heckle are quite common, somebody in the audience will just shout out some random comment or thought.

Sometimes the irrelevant heckler will want to make a statement regarding some random subject.

If you are presented with an irrelevant heckler you can combat against it with comments like

"Are you trying to heckle or just saying every word you know"

"Please save all your comments for the next therapy group".

The irrelevant heckle can be quite funny and are mostly harmless.

The Drunken Heckle.
The most common of all intended heckles and hecklers are the "Drunk".

Good luck in understanding what the drunken heckler is saying, it will normally come out as a mixture of incoherent mumbling and babbling, or be completely irrelevant.

The "Drunk" will either think he is important and / or funny, normally he will be neither.

A look at the "Heckle Lines" will give you some good ones to use. This kind of heckler is very rarely popular and can be dealt with as described in the "Dealing with Hecklers" section.

The Bored Heckle.
This type of heckle will be aimed at your show and your inability to make it interesting.

Like the abusive heckler it will normally be a single person and not the whole audience.

If you are getting a lot of these types of heckle then maybe you should look at your show and routines and maybe take the hint.

The Distraction.
This is definitely the most common form of heckle, and 99% of the time it is unintentional.

The distraction will take on many forms, more than I could list here, I will list a few that I feel are the most regular types.

People entering or exiting the venue.
This will be people calling each other, or saying goodbye. There is nothing you can do here except throw in a few quick gags, if there are people coming in, I will stop and say hello to them as well, just for the laugh.

People ordering drinks from the bar.
These things will happen and the best you can do is ride it out, by cracking a few gags or by talking over it or even asking for quiet.

People Talking.
When I put this down, a friend of mine said that a good entertainer wouldn't get people talking during their show.

If you believe this to be true then you have never been on stage.

When I went to Las Vegas I sat and watched Lance Burton and some rude people behind me just sat and talked through the whole show.

There is a great story about the American comedian Ron White. He was working in Las Vegas and during his day off he took his wife to see "Love" the Cirque Du Soleil Beatles show.

All the way through the show, all he could hear were two women behind him talking non stop, so he turned and quietly spoke to the woman and said,

"Talking during a live stage show is the height of bad manners and the social equivalent of crapping in the street".

One of the women stared at him and replied,

"You need to mind your own business".

Ron White stands up and shouts back at the women,

"You need to stop crapping in the street"

All of this during a show called "Love".

Sometimes rude people will just be rude people.

An Argument or Fight.
Believe me or not this may happen. It usually happens after a few drinks and will completely disrupt the show.

If you try and involve yourself or try and use jokes to re-establish your control of the audience then you will be putting yourself in hot water.

Not only will you become a target for the fighters, but also for any complaints from the audience that you were provoking the situation.

Leave it alone and let the establishment deal with it, then carry on with the show, however if at any time you feel your own personal safety is in jeopardy, leave the stage.

Power Cuts, Accidents or Emergencies.
Again this will happen, not very often but it will happen.

If it's a power cut, I will normally try and make light of the situation with a comment like, *"Has anyone got 10p for the meter"*.

If it is an Accident or Emergency then leave it alone, let the establishment sort it, there is nothing you can do but wait for the situation to end and then if needs be, carry on.

There are many different types of heckle, with experience you will learn some of them and more importantly how to deal with them.

Chapter Five
Performer Response Styles

The kind of responses you make will mostly depend on the style of performer you are.

If you are a serious performer and you start spouting one liners then it will not fit with your performance style.

That is not to say that you are not able to switch performance styles though. Most of the people I have chatted to regarding this book, stated they would try to deal with any situation within the style of their performance.

These categories are not mutually exclusive so you may find that you fall in two or more categories.

The King.
The King can handle any given situation and move in any direction.

He demands respect and has the ability to destroy the heckler but retain control and the respect of the audience.

This kind of response is the favourite amongst performers with heckle based acts.

Jimmy Carr is a fine example of this kind of performer.

The Joker.
Hits back with line after line, will pick up anything happening in the room and use that against the heckler.

The Joker does not believe in compromise, he will deal with the heckler and get back on with the show without stopping for breath.

The "Joker" will have a joke or line for every situation, heckle or not and will defeat any heckler without breaking a sweat.

Lee Mack is a Joker performer.

The Ninja.
The ninja is a silent assassin, he will take out his enemies without fuss or distraction.

The "Ninja" response is the "Silent" approach, no heckle lines just cold stares and sure fire body language. The heckler will feel the absolute presence and will back down.

George Carlin was a great Ninja performer.
During one show, a heckler shouted something out to George, he stopped, stared, held it for a few seconds and then carried on.

The Priest.
Calculated and clean, may use some heckle lines but none that will cause any offence, he will normally select the "Quiet" approach and likes to steer clear of any confrontational situation.
A true family performer!

Tommy Cooper fits this description.

The Politician.
Will use the "Laugh" method, and try to steer away from heckle lines until he is pushed, then the Politician will change direction and come back at the heckler with full force.

The Politician will have the audience on his side from the very beginning and because of this he won't cross the line. He will however have no intention of letting the heckler take his glory.

The Warrior.
Loud and fearless, the warrior will not take any prisoners, he will move quickly and use hard and harsh lines if need be.

The warrior is not scared of anybody and can think on his feet. The warrior has the ability to go too far and lose himself in the moment.

Check out American comedian Greg Giraldo who died in 2010 and is most famous for being part of the Comedy Central Roasts.

The Surgeon.
Remain cleaner than clean, but will use precise moves to maintain control. The Surgeon will not use heckle lines at all. The show will always be accurately thought out and any deviation will not be accepted. The surgeon will go for the "Quiet", or "Silent" approach.

The Hunter.
The hunter will set and bait his trap and allow the heckler to fall into it.

This kind of response requires a clever thinker. The hunter will lead the heckler exactly where he wants him and will finish it at the correct moment. He won't compromise the show for the sake of a quick take down.

The Buddy.
Will be the heckler's friend, he will not lose control but will take a few moments to stop and have a laugh before moving on.

The Buddy is more than happy to include the audience and is not at all perturbed by any interruption.

The Motor-Mouth.
The Motor-Mouth will completely ignore any verbal interruptions that occur and just carry on with the show. This kind of performer isn't interested in stopping his show and having a side conversation.

Ricky Gervais fits this description. I have only ever seen him respond to a heckler once, and it did not end well for the heckler.

As a performer you need to look at who you are and what your stage persona is before you choose how you wish to react.

Chapter Six
Friendly Fire

Friendly fire can come from a few directions:

- A member of the audience.
- A member of staff.

When it happens friendly banter can be a great thing.

Audience attack.
I was working in a hotel in Benidorm during the winter season of 1996. The hotel was all inclusive so there was always a lot of noise on the nights we had new arrivals. Every week on the first night some people would go a little over the top and drink a little too much.

It was about 10:30 pm, we had just finished the Cabaret show and the band was about to take over and finish the night.

At the bar was a new group of guests, and one of them was being very loud.

The gentleman was named Walter, about 45 years old and from Liverpool. He started shouting and was getting more aggravated. Eventually he was taken upstairs by his wife, but not before he nearly had a fight with his friends.

The next day I did not see Walter around the pool or at any of the daytime activities.

At about 7pm I started to begin the night time entertainment. I took a table and chair to the centre of the stage and started to get people involved as I was preparing to start the nightly fun quiz, and guess who was sat right in the front row? Walter.

Around 7.15 I started cracking jokes to the audience who were waiting and ready for the quiz.
This is something I did every night and set the atmosphere for the rest of the night.

The moment I began to talk, he began to heckle.

The first thing that struck me was, it wasn't aggressive, he was trying to be funny, and to his credit, he was a bit of a laugh.

The one thing running through my head though was I knew I had to be careful, I knew he had it in him to turn nasty.

I still had about 5 minutes before the quiz so I started some friendly banter with him.

I kept it simple, light remarks, nothing offensive.
I also tried to ad-lib some banter based around the things he was saying and doing, he always wore loud and colourful Hawaiian shirts and I made some wisecracks about them.

It was amazing, the whole audience loved it and for the next two weeks the room was packed every night for this regular addition to the show.

By controlling the situation I turned what could have been a disruption or worse, a confrontation, into something that everyone enjoyed and talked about.

To say Walter was a gift would have been an understatement. I would love to meet him now, I would shake his hand and thank him.

Now on the flip side when it comes from a member of staff you have a whole new situation to deal with.

The venue staff speaks.
When you are heckled by a member of the venue staff, this opens up a whole new arena.

First let's look at the different members of staff who may heckle.

Bar staff.
They have seen and heard every act that has come before you and will continue to see every act after you have gone.

The bar staff know the rules of the game and they are normally too busy to join in, however, if you take a poke at them, they will not be restrained in taking a poke back so best to just leave them alone and they will ignore you.

Entertainment staff.
This is where any friendly fire heckle will probably come from. Maybe from the entertainer who is the funny guy. He has a loud voice which carries above everything else or maybe he makes a comment that you hear but maybe the audience did not.

As stated above, bar staff I would avoid, even if you win, you will lose. If they heckle and you can get away with a cheeky line, then great, but if it is not said in the lightest of ways, you could face trouble.

If you are heckled by the entertainment staff, and it is good natured and you can use it, then use it.

If you have an act that allows a distraction such as this, then you have been given a gift, you can create a moment, one that is off the cuff and in the eyes of the audience a golden moment.

This is what the audience loves to see, interaction between their entertainers, who they support night after night of their holiday, and the guest act.

People love watching outtakes of movies for exactly that reason, they love to see the interaction, the off the beaten track stuff. You can now deliver that to them in whatever manner you decide.

Keep it nice, fun, and entertaining and you have won the audience for the rest of the show, and the entertainers for the rest of the season and beyond.

I have even taught the entertainers a trick, something simple with a change bag for example, so that when I return to the venue, and when they heckle again, I can get them up, in the view of making fun of them, but actually turning them into the star, by enabling them to take the applause.

No presumptions.
As I entered the bar one evening 150 British Army and RAF troops were sitting all around the bar, they were a talkative group and I got chatting to them before I went to get ready for the show.

One of them started telling me how they travel on ships a lot and that they are going to rip me apart, how they love to destroy the magicians on these ships and that I am next on their list.

I decided that I have heard enough and I headed backstage and started to prepare, trying to decide on which lines to use, what tricks I have that I can use to my advantage.

By the time I headed onto the stage I was a bag of nerves, I tried to remain calm and decide that I was just going to go for it and no one was going to stop me.

I walked onto the stage, one of the troops gave me a line and I instantly started a line of banter with him.

Nothing heavy or too hard, just a few lines about his uniform being creased, he needed a shave and also how young he looked. He was one of the younger troops so I incorporated an older soldier using the line,

"He was on the front gate, when you were on cow and gate".

Before I knew it, I had all the troops clapping and screaming. They really loved the show, heckling to my advantage and allowing me to get the big laughs.

Looking back it was definitely one of my favourite nights.

Chapter Seven
Enemy Fire

Not all banter is friendly, sometimes you will have to deal with people who just want to shout abuse at you.

The main difference between this and friendly fire is the hostile intent.

Normally the heckles will be directed at you personally, they may however just be a desire from someone for you to get off, or get the dancing girls back on.

My tips for Enemy Fire:

- Stay in control. Keep your voice strong, it's your show and you must remain in charge.

- Keep responses short and simple.

- Remember that you are a professional and you should act as one at all times.

- Don't get dragged into a side conversation that will disrupt the flow of the show, deal with it and move on.

- Be aware of the lines you use. You may lose the audience if they were unaware that the heckler was being annoying, to them it may have just been some "Friendly Banter".

- Above all, do not lose control.

Chapter Eight
The Double Decker

The "Double Decker" is my term for when another heckler joins in.

Sometimes you will be half way through dealing with a heckler and for some unknown reason, a completely different person starts to heckle.

This is a serious problem and can escalate. You need to quickly and efficiently deal with the original heckler, stop the new heckler and make sure that nobody else gets the same idea and starts to heckle as well.

If dealt with incorrectly the audience will turn on you and there will be little chance of a comeback.

Let us say a "Double Decker" has happened, before you can respond to the heckle you must evaluate why it happened.

Was it your fault?
If it was your fault, you must rectify it, if you are able.

If it was something you have said or done, then you need to either move the show on and away from the incident or respond in a way that does not inflame the situation more.

Is it a rough audience?
If it is a rough audience they may heckle anyway, but at least you can prepare yourself for it beforehand.

From the answers to the first two questions you should now be able to answer the third question.

Is there any possibility that others may join in?

These questions need to be answered before you take on the hecklers.

The second heckler is in the equation now, but you must control the situation so others don't follow suit.

The second heckler will fall under two categories:

- They know the original heckler.

- They don't know the original heckler.

If they know each other, then you may have to deal with them in the way that you would a "Group", (see group hecklers next chapter).

If they don't know each other or you feel that method will not work then you have to take a different approach.

You should have already categorised the first heckler.

Now categorise the second heckler.

Next you must decide which of the two hecklers is more dangerous and deal with them first.

Be prepared to switch heckler though, the first heckler you take on may well ease up and the other heckler intensify.

Don't continually switch back and forth, this will cause confusion amongst the audience and you will lose them.

Remember that only some of the audience will be able to hear what is being said by the heckler. Most of the audience will only hear what you say.

If you need to switch, then do it, ideally you need to deal with one completely and then, if the other heckler is still going you are now in a better position to deal with him and carry on with the show.

If you are using heckle lines then a quick line at the very beginning of the situation will establish that you are still in control, a good line is,

"What is this a tag team?"

Use the situation and get a laugh, this will buy you a few seconds to evaluate and make a decision.

This can sometimes defuse one or both hecklers, and cause them both to quieten down. They have had their laugh and you have not resorted to belittling them.

One tactic I like to use in these situations is to adopt a different method from the one I am using on the first heckler.

For instance if I am using lines against the first heckler I will go for the laugh approach with the second, with the correct wording this can have the effect that the second heckler is backing me up,

"*Yeah mate, I know what you mean*".

It may not make sense to the second heckler but odds are that the audience didn't even hear the second heckle, and the first heckler now thinks the audience has turned against him.

Remember you have different tactics at your disposal, use them to your advantage.

If you should be heckled again, be aware of the position of the original "Double Deckers", they may well want to join in again and you should be ready for them.

Remember you can only use each heckle line once in a show, and you may have already used some of your best material earlier on.

Chapter Nine
The Group

Dealing with groups of people is always difficult but it doesn't need to be a problem.

We have to take a look at the information on hand to tell us the best way to deal with the situation.

1. What kind of group are they?

2. Why are the group talking and not watching?

3. Can you get them to stop talking and start watching?

4. If you can't stop them, can you at least quieten them?

What kind of group are they?
Just like the individual heckler, the group has to be classified, however here you can easily spot what kind of group they are.

- Are they younger or older?
- Are they a stag or hen group?
- Is it a group of friends?
- Is it work mates, or a company event?
- Are they same sex, or mixed?
- Are they all drunk?
- Are some of them drunk?

Why are they talking and not watching?
Well this could be caused by any number of reasons.

- They are on a bar crawl, stag or hen or some sort of special event.
- They are not interested in your show.
- They are bored.
- They are drunk.
- They are just plain rude.
- All or a mixture of the above.

Can you get them to stop talking and start watching?
This you will have to decide for yourself under the circumstances at the time.

You may find that pointing some banter their way will be enough to get them on side, or you may find they just don't care or are not interested and ignore you for the rest of the show.

If you can't stop them, can you at least quieten them?
Again this will depend on the circumstances you are in.
You have to be careful not to enrage them, from their point of view they are in the venue for their party.
To the room as a whole you are the main event but to the group you are just noise in the background.

If you start verbally attacking a noisy group, they could turn nasty for a couple of reasons:

- They may not have realised just how noisy they have been.
- You have asked them to quieten down and they have had a few drinks.
- They are idiots who only think of themselves and do not care about the rest of the rooms' enjoyment.
- They will see this as an unprovoked attack, and will turn their anger towards you, this will include an increase in their volume (much louder than they were already being).

This is not a good situation to be facing.

I have in the past, tried to engage with the group.
Some simple techniques include:

- Asking where they are from?

- Asking what they are celebrating?

I was once dealing with a birthday group,
so I asked

"Please can I have a slice of cake?"

The groups alpha male (who was tall and very, very skinny), replied,

"You look like you have had enough cake mate".

He got a nice laugh, including one from me before I hit him back with,

"You look like you have to run around in the shower to get wet".

The whole room erupted, including his group.

The next thing I saw was him, walking towards the stage with a plate and a giant piece of cake.

I quickly said,

"Please do not throw it at me, I will have to duck, and that is considered exercise".

Another big laugh and he smiled, placed the cake on the edge of the stage, smiled again and walked away.

The cake was yummy, just in case you wondered.

Generally though the best way to deal with this group is to just ignore it and carry on, remember it may seem loud to you on stage, but maybe your voice or music is louder to the audience.

The other method is to ask one of the staff to just pop over and have a word, the venue staff are normally adept at dealing with these groups and may already know the people and be in a much better situation to quieten them down.

Not all "Group" stories have a happy ending.

Group Hell
On one of the ships I worked we used to get booze cruisers, groups of people heading for a wild weekend on the continent.

I walked on stage to be met by 15 middle-aged men. They were sitting near the stage and started shouting abuse as soon as I walked on. They were really going for it, non stop abuse for 45 minutes.

No matter what lines I used, or what tactics I employed they just kept going.

I tried to get them on-side, I tried to turn it into a positive but they just wanted to destroy the act.

At one point the audience turned against them, telling them to be quiet, but to no avail.

I finished my time on stage and took what applause there was, not my best performance.

Remember you can't win them all.

Chapter Ten
The Microphone Grabber

The Microphone Grabber is anybody who approaches you while on stage and either grabs at or asks for the microphone.

If handled properly, this will be one of the easier hecklers to deal with.

First let's look at why people do this and then I will give you my way of dealing with it.

- They are drunk and want to talk to the audience or start telling their own jokes, but much more likely they will want to sing.

- They want to speak to the audience, usually an announcement, *"My mate is 46 tomorrow, can we all sing happy birthday to her".*

- They want to ask the audience a question.

What happens now is the most crucial part, this is so important, it's simple common sense, but unfortunately common sense isn't as common as it should be. Remember, no matter what the circumstances

NEVER HAND OVER THE MICROPHONE.

It's the end of the line if you do. It's the touch of death to any act for a member of the audience to get a hold of the microphone.
You wouldn't let anyone touch any of your props or equipment, and the microphone is no exception.

Once that microphone is in the hand of the heckler anything can and will happen, they will almost certainly start shouting, singing and worst of all swearing; once you lose that microphone you have lost everything.

How do you deal with this?
The best way to deal with this is simple but very effective.

You are on stage and during your show you see the person approaching you.

Lean forward and put your hand with the microphone, behind your back.

The microphone should be in the middle of your back running along your spine.

You are now between the heckler and the microphone, no matter how hard they try to grab the microphone by using your body as a shield they will be unable to reach it.

This means that the person has to speak to you and ask to use the microphone.

You have maintained **control**, and you now have the opportunity to evaluate the situation and decide the best course of action.

They will either give up and walk away muttering under their breath or tell you what they want to say.
It is now up to you.

If it's a birthday or special announcement I tell the person that I will announce it and get a good applause for it.

If it's a wannabe singer, I tell them that it's not possible and to return back to their seats or refer them to the entertainments team at the side of the stage who can answer any questions they have about the planning of the karaoke.

Any good venue will have staff on hand to deal with people who take to the stage, however if not, it is up to you to maintain a strong position, make it clear they will not get the microphone and they are to return to their seats.

Remember.
Keep your voice strong and confident, be polite not rude, firm but fair, you are in charge and you are not about to let that situation change.

If the heckler persists, ask for assistance from the venue staff.

If the person starts to get physical, walk off stage straight away.

Remember:
NEVER HAND OVER THE MICROPHONE.

Chapter Eleven
When Venue Staff Attack

Staff attack.
I was on stage at a holiday park, about to do an effect called the bill switch, the basic premise is that one bank note (in my case £20 borrowed from the audience) changes to a $1 bill.

As the effect happens a voice from the side of me shouts out "I have seen this trick before, it uses a plastic thumb."

I looked around and the voice who shouted it out was none other than one of the entertainment staff, who was now happily telling everyone around her, in her nice clear voice where to look and what it was.

Now for starters this is completely unprofessional behaviour, the staff at these venues are privy to magic effect methods, as they see you set up your act and also watch the act, week after week, month after month.

Now some people are just thick, they speak without thinking and do not have to bear any consequences, because it is not their act they have just ruined.

This is a very awkward situation to find yourself in, and one that does not really have a happy ending.

The first thing you have to decide is whether you are going to say anything there and then.

Can you get away with verbally attacking a member of the venue staff?

Personally I think this is career suicide, unless they have done something so heinous that you do not mind losing this work forever. (I once saw an entertainer start a fight and throw a glass at the bartender at one lovely holiday camp in Kent).

This may be one of those situations that you have to take on the chin and carry on.

You can complain, but what good will that do, you will almost certainly not work at that park or venue again, and that then puts a mark against your name for any other venue in the same company.

My course of action was to have a word with the entertainer openly in a nice way after the gig.

I was packing up, she came backstage and was saying how much she enjoyed the show, I just mentioned that in future it would probably be better if she did not mention how the tricks were done. She laughed and agreed with me.

This situation is completely unfair to the performer, luckily it is a situation that does not arise too often.

Chapter Twelve
The Act Assassin

The ultimate heckler and heckles.

The hit.
You are on stage, the heckler has you in his sights he shouts something at you, you respond and suddenly "Bam" you have just lost.

It's as simple and as quick as that. The heckler has said something and before you even register what it is, it's over.

You start to sweat and look around you for some sort of support.

The audience are jeering and now you have other people heckling you, although you can't make out the words as your brain is in hyperdrive but coming up blank.

You start to panic and feel a bit sick, all your worst fears have happened at once.

The MC is looking at you for some sort of signal. You have nowhere to turn and no one to help you.

The audience has turned on you and start to boo and hiss, someone starts a chant,

"OFF, OFF, OFF, OFF, OFF, OFF, OFF, OFF".

Not nice and it leaves a terrible feeling in your stomach.

It has not happened to me but I saw it happen once, and I am so pleased it was not aimed at me.

A true "Act Assassin" is extremely RARE, but they do happen.

There are two types of "Act Assassin".

- The lucky hitter.
- The professional assassin.

The lucky hitter.
This will be someone who says the right thing at the right time, he will say something that just slays you.

He may not mean it to, but once done, it's done.

The odds of this happening are very low though, you have many factors on your side like noise, attention etc.

The heckler has to be heard by all or most of the audience and also more importantly understood, however with the right timing and the right voice it can happen.

You have been warned.

The professional assassin.
This guy is more likely. He gets his kicks from doing this as often as he can, his heckles will be twice as strong, destructive and will inflict maximum damage.

He has worked on lines and manipulates situations, especially in venues where you may be regularly booked and he knows your act.

I have seen them destroy the confidence of the performer and kill the act completely.

You can stop it, right up until the moment that it happens, then it's too late and there is nothing you can do.

When it does happen, it will be so fast that you won't know what hit you, one minute you are doing your normal show, the next you're getting laughed off stage, all your self-respect destroyed and confidence blown.

So how do you deal with this?

If it's a true assassin heckle and they are calling for you to get off the stage, then that may be your only course of action and you put it down to experience and hope that it won't come back to haunt you with other bookers.

My all time favorite story, and one that I try and tell at every opportunity is this one.

I was booked to perform for a family group at a hospice charity fundraising event. I was booked to do 15-20 minutes of family magic and to compere the rest of the show.

I was followed by a dancing girl with a ribbon on a stick, she was asked to do an 8-10 minute set and another magician, this time aimed at the children who were asked to do a 20 minute spot.

The audience was comprised of approximately 150 children, some of whom were patients at the hospice, their brothers and sisters, plus around 200 adults.

Some of the children were in very poor health, but this did not mean they were not ready to enjoy a show.

In the front row was a little boy, aged around 9, in a wheelchair. His chair was hooked up with monitors and electrodes, he had a drip and it was very clear that he was very, very poorly.

He had an Ironman t-shirt on and I mentioned that I had mistaken him for Tony Stark in his suit and he laughed as did his dad who was sitting next to him.

I did my show, it went down well, the dancer also did a good job, and we both received good ovations.

The second magician came on and started his act.

This magician was using a classic Supreme Magic children's prop called the "Crown Jewels".

Any children's magician will tell you that with this prop, you can do 5 minutes or 45 minutes. This magician decided to do the latter.

Around 40 minutes into his supposed 20 minute set, the children were getting restless. He was milking the effect to the very limit.

The venue staff were annoyed as he had over run by so much time and the audience too were getting frustrated as he was repeating the effect over and over.

This little boy had clearly had enough and turned to his dad, and said in a voice that carried above the microphone and all across the room,

"Dad, I do not think I will live long enough to see the end of this trick".

The room erupted, the magician had no options and after a few moments left the stage.

One of my other favourite stories is kind of an act assassin even though the comedian brought it on himself, let me explain.

Kirk Douglas's son Eric, half brother to legendary actor Michael, had been trying his hand at comedy.

He wasn't that bad and had managed to get himself a 30 minute spot at a London comedy club.

The crowd that night were not a forgiving group however and he was dying a death, people were heckling and he was getting more and more frustrated until finally he snapped and shouted into the microphone,

"Dammit, you can not do this to me, don't you people know who I am, I am Kirk Douglas's son".

At this point the main heckler in the front row jumped up and shouted,

"NO, I am Kirk Douglas's son",

referring to the iconic "I'm Spartacus" scene of the 1960 film starring Kirk Douglas.

Within seconds everyone was on their feet shouting the same thing. I was told that people were still shouting it five minutes after he had left the stage.

You may notice a similarity in the two stories above, in both situations the attitude of the performer was ultimately the main reason for his downfall.

If the first performer had stuck to the rules, done the correct amount of time and got off when he was supposed to, the situation would never have arisen.

If Eric had maintained his composure, earned their respect rather than demanding it and not panicked, he may well have survived the situation with some dignity.

Chapter Thirteen
Damien

Being heckled by an adult is one thing, however if a child heckles you, then it is a completely different game.

Most parents will respond when asked to quieten their children, but unfortunately some parents are under the impression that you are in fact a babysitter and that they can leave their children with you while they sit and chat loudly at the bar.

This can even happen in an environment that is not a family one.

The family show.
In this situation the children will normally be sat with their parents, or on chairs or on the floor in front of you and the parents sat at tables behind.

If a child is interrupting you, then you must deal with them in a professional but strong manner.

Be nice, kind, but speak in a firm voice as you say something along the lines of,

"Sit quietly for me kids".

This does not single out one child but instead speaks to them as a group.

If he carries on I will single out the child and say,

"Quiet please, you are ruining the show for everyone else".

At this point most parents will intervene and tell the child to sit properly. If the problem continues I will then ask for the parents to remove the child to their tables or seats.

If the child is sat with their parents and starts to shout out, you can just follow the same procedure as above and ask for quiet or if they do nothing then a quick line like,

"Can we plug his chair in?"

This will put the attention on their table and the parents will quieten the child.

If this doesn't work, obviously you are moving into a dangerous area, the parents either do not care or can not control their child and it is now becoming a situation that could destroy your show.

The child will continue to shout and disrupt, because he thinks he has beaten you already.

In this instance, I usually find that speaking to the parents off microphone will suffice or just ignore the child.

I further distance myself by making sure that any assistants I require will be chosen from the other side of the audience for the remainder of the show, allowing me to totally ignore the child.

If you decide to start a barrage of lines or abuse at the table you will almost definitely lose the audience and that's a route you do not want to take.

The adult / blue show.
If you perform in an adult environment, and there are children present then the parents must accept and respect that the show is booked for the intended audience.

If you do find yourself in this position, the only thing you can do is make an announcement or have the compere make an announcement at the beginning.

Remember that you are there to perform your act, and not to deal with a 6-year-old child that makes Damien look like Annie.

Always stay professional and in charge and everything will be fine.

I learnt a lot from watching teachers and the way they talk to their students.

A good teacher doesn't have to raise their voice to keep control; they use a simple technique.

Change the tone of your voice, make it a little sterner and look straight into the eyes of the child as you ask them to sit down and be quiet.

It is a great skill to learn.

So what kinds of child hecklers are there?

The annoying, the attention deficient and the spoilt child.
These three can all be dealt with by following the above method.

The crying child.
Not a lot can be done here; I will sometimes ask if everything is alright?

This puts the attention on the parents and 99% of the time gets them to control the child. If however they do not, there is little that can be done.

One thing I do is speak softly to the child, this sometimes is enough to stop the crying but not always.
If they carry on crying, I will normally crack a joke like, "I do kid's shows too".

The drunken child.
This is a hard one to deal with, obviously the parents do not care or they have no control over the child and allow them to do whatever they want.

Your best choice of action is to follow the above advice. The audience will normally back you up here. Normal people do not like to see a drunken child and this allows you a little extra freedom.

I will normally throw in a few "Drunk" lines as well, mainly to emphasize the stupidity of the parents for allowing it.

The demon child.
The demon child is the worst sort of child, normally aged between 8 and 13 this child is best described as a combination of all of the above and unfortunately uncontrollable by most parents.

Recently I have had the misfortune to discover that most demon children learn their skills from their parents.

This can cause many problems especially when the parent starts giving you abuse for making fun of their child.

My normal route is to start some gentle banter with the parents, a few well chosen softer gags to keep them on side will normally get them to maintain some level of discipline with the demon as they do not want to be embarrassed in front of the rest of the group.

Be careful though, sometimes the parents can use this as an excuse to attack, remember the child learns from the parent, they may be worse than the child.

This leads me to the next main point:

DO NOT GET THIS CHILD UP TO HELP

This is the worst mistake, if you get the demon child up, you are basically inviting them to take over.

The demon child has no respect for anyone, this includes authority figures such as teachers, their own parents and especially you.

Damien & Co.
I was performing close up magic in the piano bar on one of the ships I have worked on.

I had performed to one table which consisted of the father, mother, two teenage boys about fourteen years old, and their daughter who was about eight.

The table was quite responsive and I carried on performing around the bar area.

After about thirty minutes the father, mother and daughter left the bar and left the two boys with some other lads who had joined the table, as I was finishing at the table I was on, one of the boys shouts at me across the bar,

"Oi, Boy come show us some more tricks"

I wish I could say that I had some quick witted response to this, I decided to ignore him, pretend I hadn't heard him and moved on to the next desired table.

My favourite bit was the "Oi, Boy", I must confess that I did very briefly think of using the line,

"Boy! Boy! I am old enough to be your dad, in fact I nearly was but I didn't have the correct change".

Looking back, I am quite glad that I didn't.

Chapter Fourteen
Body Language

This chapter will explore the importance of being able to read and recognise the heckler's body language and how the body language you use impacts the situation.

The hecklers body language.
For the most part you may only be able to see the top half of the hecklers body.

They will either be sat at a table or behind someone else, unless they are sat in the front row or in an exposed position, so you need to look at the face, head and shoulders to get most of the information you will require to read the heckler.

When people are happy or laughing, you can tell what they are thinking, they will be smiling and laughing.

When people are angry or unhappy with you, you will see unconscious facial expressions and body language aimed at you.

These facial expressions are known as "Micro Expressions" and for more information I highly recommend all of the books by Dr Paul Eckman including "Emotions Revealed" and "Emotion in the human face" which cover many of the skills required in this chapter.

Anger.
Anger is probably the easiest to spot.

We have all had someone angry at us, whether it is a teacher at school or the old guy who is annoyed we parked our car outside his house.

Anger is normally displayed hard and fast, the eyes will narrow, squint and normally carry a hard cold stare too.

This is an evolutionary trait, it allows us to track a target and focus on the take down.

People who express anger will also narrow their eyebrows and tighten their lips.

Alongside these facial expressions you may well see these "Indicators".

Typical indicators will be aimed at you, even though the angry heckler may well be talking to someone else at the time.

- Snarling
- Hand swatting
- Pointing and jabbing

Snarling.
When a dog snarls, it clenches its teeth, exposes the teeth and breathes heavily. This is identical when a person does it.

Hand swatting.
Like flicking away a fly or insect, normally done in the direction of the person they are talking about.

Pointing and jabbing.
As the person is berating you to whoever will listen, they will point at you, for extra emphasis they may further express anger by jabbing their fingers in your direction.

The performer's body language.
How you are seen whilst performing, and especially how you are seen when you are dealing with a situation is crucial to how the situation will resolve.

Look at how you stand, how you use your hands and body to express what you are saying and doing.

Someone standing with their hands in their pockets, or someone who is continually looking at their feet, will not inspire confidence, but if that same person was standing tall, shoulders back, not slouching and showing confidence will place you in a position of authority.

When I walk on stage, I open my arms to the side and turn my palms outwards in a gesture of welcome, and I smile.

Showing your palms is a gesture of trust and openness and of course smiling is, well it's just nice.

Chapter Fifteen
Controlling The Banter

What is Banter?

banter
/ˈbantə/

noun
1. the playful and friendly exchange of teasing remarks.
"there was much good-natured banter"

verb
1. exchange remarks in a good-humoured teasing way.
"the men bantered with the waitresses"

When you are having a friendly and funny conversation with an audience member it is called banter.

Speaking to the audience and asking where people are from is banter.

The use of heckle-lines and the responses are banter.

Friendly banter (friendly fire) can be a great thing and some audiences expect it, so you must be ready for it and know what to do when it does happen. This will happen a lot in venues such as holiday parks.

Unfriendly banter (enemy fire) can be devastating if not dealt with correctly.

Some acts do not allow for any banter with the audience, whilst some rely on it to make their act work.

Dara O'Briain is a great example of a comedian who uses banter to lead him into his next section, giving his shows an almost impromptu feel about them.

So how do we control the banter?

How do we make sure we maintain control over what is said and what is done?

If the routine calls for you to interact with a spectator then controlling banter is very important, it comes down to control over the audience.

Keep to the routine and interact with the audience member as much or as little as you can control.

Give too much and the audience member could get excited and ruin the moment but give too little and you may not get the required response from the audience member.

You also need to maintain some self discipline here too. It is very easy to lose yourself in the moment and carry the banter too far.

Chapter Sixteen
Responding

With all the hecklers the secret is not to let them visibly see that they have succeeded in disrupting you. You should appear as if everything is running exactly as planned.

The heckler is nothing to you, and you are not going to let them ruin your show.

When a person heckles you, should you respond?
In recent years we have seen an outpouring of programs like X-factor, The Voice and the well known talent show and in these shows the audience is expected to contribute to the basic feeling of the audience, they are encouraged to boo or cheer as to influence the tempo of the show.

This has always been a part of live performance but now some people think they have the right to interact with the performer and they do not seem to realise that it is not a controlled environment like a TV show and the performer will interact back.

- So is this right?
- Should we be getting involved?
- Should we just get on with the job at hand?

Let us break this down to both sides of the argument.

The argument for yes.
If someone is deliberately trying to disrupt your show then the answer must be, "Yes"

No other occupation would allow someone to be abusive towards them and interrupt, so why should you?

Unfortunately there are some people who are so rude that they feel that they have the right to shout out during your performance.

You should deal with these people, but you must make sure that it is in a professional manner, as long as you can maintain control of the audience and can deal with the situation without compromising the pace, tempo and standard of the show.

The argument for no.
Is it really what an audience wants to see?

If you do get into a verbal confrontation then it will come down to 2 possible outcomes: a winner and a loser.

If you lose.
Not only do you look incompetent but you also end up losing the respect of the entire audience.

If you Win.
Then you have insulted an audience member, you have had to belittle someone to the point of smugness.

Is it right for you to make your audience sit through a battle of wits between a random spectator and a supposed professional?

You should not get yourself into that situation in the first place.

You need to stay in control of your show and don't let any comments distract you, the audience will probably not even hear what the heckler says so don't lower yourself to their level.

The Answer.
The final decision comes down to you.

You need to take a long look at yourself, your personality, your audience and your show and make a decision on how you will deal with a heckler if you should encounter one.

Sometimes you may want to have some banter but it would not be appropriate, or you may not feel like the timing is correct.

Evaluate and respond appropriately.

Chapter Seventeen
Using Heckle Lines

Some people do not like the idea of using heckle lines or put downs. If someone heckles you, and you want to use lines you have to let events run a certain course.

If you come straight out with your most abusive line, it may well stop him dead in his tracks, but you will also lose any respect with the audience.

You must build up to it, so that when you do, the audience back you 100%.

So what do you do?

What is the first line that will show this upstart that you are not going to take his lame ignorant insults?

How will you demonstrate what a funny, quick witted not to be messed with kinda performer you are?

I always use this one:

"Excuse me"

Okay so it's no show stopper but from these two words I learn a lot from the person that is heckling.

Almost enough to tell which of the heckler's I am dealing with!

If he repeats what he said.
He is not the Hardcore, who would have known that a good heckle depends on timing.

By repeating what was said, he has missed the moment, therefore the comment is no longer relevant and no longer funny.

From this information you can determine that he is probably the "Would Be" or "The Drunk" and you should deal with as such.

61

If he doesn't repeat what he said.
The heckler may be embarrassed by the fact that you actually responded to him (sometimes they don't think you will hear or respond to the heckle).

Maybe he is a coward and doesn't have the courage to repeat what he said.

Another reason he didn't respond is that he understands the concept of comedy and knows that he will just look stupid if he repeats.

If this is the case then you are probably looking at the "The Comic", "Hardcore" or a tuned in "Would be".

"The Drunk" will almost always repeat

Whether they repeat or not I usually follow that line with

"That's great thanks"

Again not a killer line but you are still in control.

At this point in the interruption I feel I have reached a crossroad. I can go left or right or carry on.

By following what I have said I have chosen to go straight ahead, I haven't changed direction and I haven't made fun of anyone. I have remained in control and by staying professional I can carry on with my show.

If the heckler persists then … well we will come to that.

If you choose to respond straight away it can narrow the choices later on, for instance, some of the audience may not even have heard the heckle line so it might look like you are insulting a member of the audience for cheap laughs, stay on top and let the heckler dig his own hole.

One of the main secrets to dealing with a heckler is not to let it show that they have fazed you. By using the above method you can also stop the heckler before he can really begin.

By dismissing both the negative comment and his attempts to disrupt, sometimes the heckler will simply give up, not always but it does sometimes happen.

Using this method also gives you a few seconds to gather your thoughts, address the situation and decide where you want to go with it.

So let's assume you have decided to use heckle lines, you are now entering a different style of performance and you must stick to the rules of engagement or you will become the bad guy.

Heckle lines should never be delivered in a mean or aggressive way. When you use a heckle line you are making fun of them, insulting them, you are attacking their:

- Sexuality
- Intellect
- Social ability
- Job
- Looks
- Number of friends
- Family
- Upbringing
- Wealth
- Fashion sense

The wrong person can, and possibly will take offence and that can lead to the types of problems and situations you would really rather prefer to stay clear from. (see crossing the line).

Remember this is not personal, it is just someone in the audience speaking out.

The military rules of engagement:

- *You have the right to use force to defend yourself against attacks or threats of attack.*
- *Hostile fire may be returned to stop a hostile act.*
- *When troops are attacked by unarmed hostile elements, use minimum force proportional to the threat.*
- *Treat all persons with dignity and respect.*
- *Be prepared to act in self defence*

A quick Google search or look on Wikipedia will find hundreds of thousands of pages on the subject of the rules of engagement, it is very informative and worth a look and a read.

Let's now look at how we can adapt this for our purposes.

Firstly you will not require automatic weapons or any close quarter combat ability.

The stage rules of engagement:

- You have the right to defend yourself against attacks or threats of attack.
- Heckle lines should only be used when necessary.
- When attacked by any hostile elements, use reasonable return fire, proportional to the threat.
- Treat all persons with dignity and respect.
- Be professional.
- Be nice, until it is time not to be nice.
- Stay in control.
- Smile.

Remember, you are responsible for what you do and say on stage.

Do not use any lines that are outside of what you can handle.

If at any time you feel threatened or unsafe, leave the stage.

Making the punishment fit the crime.
The heckles that you deliver must be consistent with what is happening in relation to the heckler.

There is no point using "Drunk" lines on a heckler who is not drunk.

I once saw this exact situation happen when a comedian in a club reacted to a very sober man with the line,

"Go sit by the wall, that is plastered too".

The line was completely out of context with the situation and failed to hit any mark, because there was no mark to hit.

This comedian failed, because he was not aware of what was happening around him.

The heckle came, and instead of taking a second or two, so he could assess the situation, and then reply, he panicked and just threw the first line that he thought of at the heckler.

Know the heckler before you deal with the heckler.

Chapter Eighteen
Heckle Lines

Regular lines.
Why don't you slip into something more comfortable like a coma?

Every time he drinks water, the toilet seat bangs the back of his head.

How long do you have to wear that suit until you win the bet?

How would you like it if I came to McDonald's and kicked the mop out of your hand?

It's a night out for you, but a night off for your care assistant.

Hey, I like doing my act the way you like having
sex, alone.

You can go home now, the cage should be cleaned out by now.

I will ignore you, it's be kind to animals week.

Is this your first time heckling?

Save your next comment for your therapy group.

You are not one in a million, won in a raffle more like.

Hold your breath for a minute and make me happy, better still hold your breath for an hour and make everyone happy.

Bet your jaws are happy when you sleep.

He has a photographic memory, too bad it never developed.

It's nice that you gave us a piece of your mind, especially as you have so little to spare.

You have the kind of face that grows on you, I am just glad it didn't grow on me.

You're about as useful as a chocolate fire guard.

Sorry mate I don't do requests.

Are you trying to heckle or are you just shouting all the words you know.

A mind is a terrible thing to waste.

Could you take your breakdown somewhere else?

Is there a name for what's wrong with you?

Can't swim, can't keep his mouth shut long enough.

Can't put on make-up, she can't keep her mouth shut long enough.

There is a bus in 5 minutes mate, be under it.

I do free shows in aid of people like him.

He must have a sixth sense, he doesn't have any sign of the other five.

Can I have your head for my rock garden?

He should be buried at least 100 ft underground, deep down he is a good person.

You remind me of the River Thames, wide at the mouth and full of rubbish.

Was it cold on the floor this morning?

As an outsider, what do you think of the human race?

You have that far away look, the further away you are, the better you look.

If you were that important the audience would be facing you.

I have seen wounds dressed better than you.

I am trying to picture you with a personality.

Act like a man or don't you do impressions.

That's care in the community for you.

That's what happens when cousins marry.

He is an authority with the ladies, the ladies don't know but the authorities certainly do.

He is a Don Juan with the ladies.
They Don Juan (don't want) to know him.

I like your approach, now lets see your departure.

Here's 10p go phone all your friends and bring back the change.

You would make a great goalie for the darts team.

The wheel is spinning but the hamster is dead.

The gates are down, the lights are flashing, but I think the train is delayed.

Nice suit, did the clown die?

I wish I could afford to buy enough wood to board up your mouth.

You're a card, shame it's not the joker.

After the show a motorcycle daredevil will attempt to jump his mouth.

At least when he is talking he isn't thinking.

Looks like Snow White and Dopey had a kid after all.

You shouldn't be heckling me, your brain is too tense.
'Two tenth's' the size of a normal brain.

He has a kind face, the kind you want to smash through the window.

Come on mate laugh, I did when you walked in.

I have seen you on TV, interference.

You remind me of a bunch of roses, there's always one prick in every bunch.

Have you seen playschool? You are going through the square window.

I wouldn't let your mind wander, it's too small to go out on its own.

We could have a battle of wits, but you are unarmed.

Can we plug his chair in?

(Loud shirt) Nice shirt, keep wearing it, it might come back in fashion.

You have a ready wit, let me know when it's ready.

His elevator doesn't go to the top floor.

Go on mate tell me everything you know, I have a few seconds to kill.

I'll help you out, which way did you come in.

If wit were chocolate you wouldn't have enough to fill an M&M.

He is very down to earth, just not down far enough.

Are you from the shallow end of the gene pool?

You are funny, you should get an agent.
A travel agent and go somewhere else.

If he went to a mind reader he would get 50% off.

If he went to a mind reader he would get his money back.

We have some bad news tonight, the first is that the toilets are not working tonight, the second is that this blokes mouth is.

Who gave you a speaking part.

Whatever you are drinking, save some for me.

You must have loads of money, you don't spend it on your clothes.

Calling you stupid would be an insult to stupid people.

Do you ever wonder what life would be if you hadn't been deprived of oxygen at birth?

Do you still love nature, despite what it's done to you?

Female Heckler
She was nicer to me in the toilet.

How can you look so clean and laugh so dirty?

You would look good in something flowing, like a river.

How many peeping Tom's have you cured?

Drunk
Remember the good old days?
When alcoholics were anonymous.

Close your mouth mate, if someone lights a cigarette the whole place could go up.

Can you slur that again?

Alcohol abuse is a terrible thing.

Instant idiot, just add alcohol.

I remember my first pint.

Never drink on an empty head.

Go stand by the wall mate, that's plastered as well.

Chapter Nineteen
Not Using Heckle Lines

So how do you deal with the different heckler's without using heckle lines?

Not all people are comfortable using heckle lines, maybe you feel that your act doesn't accommodate the further distraction of engaging a conversation with the heckler.

Some people just do not want to engage with the audience in this manner, so what is the alternative?

There are ways and means of handling the situation. Let's have a look at a couple of options that you have.

The laugh approach.
Just a quick laugh and *"Cheers for that"* or *"Thanks for sharing"*, and then carry on.

It shows that you are not about to start a character battle and that any further attempts will be met with a similar dismissive manner.

This I feel is one of the most popular and effective methods.

Whilst researching I spoke to performers, some who did and some who didn't use lines, most agreed that this would be their first method of dealing with the heckler.
If it failed then they would move the level up a notch.

The silent approach.
Just ignore them, give them a couple of disapproving looks, you are there to do your show, not make one up with a random audience member.

You have the microphone and the other guy doesn't so after a few failed attempts to get a response without success they will most likely give up.

The quiet approach.
Ask them to be quiet, tell them they are ruining the show for the other people and that it will not be tolerated.

They should respect the people watching the show. If they continue to heckle, stop the show, ask them again to be quiet, give them a slightly off look, wait for them to be quiet, then carry on.

If they continue, stop again, by isolating them they have failed to turn the audience against you and be more popular than you are, and will back off.

The beforehand approach.
This can be very effective, before the show, some performers will speak to the management of the venue, and ask that if anyone interrupts to have them dealt with.

In recent years I have seen a lot of comedy venues, and entertainment venues develop a no heckling policy

They spend so much money on the acts they don't want some idiot in the front row trying to take over and they deal quite harshly with them, including removing and banning them from the bar.

What is nice here is that if one method doesn't work then just try another.

You haven't upset or offended anyone with these approaches so just switch tactics and if need be just switch back again later. Sometimes a combination of attacks can be the best defence.

From experience, when I have used these methods I would start with the "**Laugh**", then move onto the "**Silent**" and then finally onto the "**Quiet**". This is a nice progressive course that intensifies each time.

It will depend on which heckler you are dealing with as to which approach you take.

The heckler isn't going to be as polite as you, but by being prepared you are going to rise above him and guide the audience away from the distraction.

The main benefit of not using hecklines is that you can change your mind and use them later on in the performance.

It also means you will definitely not be crossing the line or upsetting anyone. It is the safest option by far.

Chapter Twenty
If They Carry On Heckling

Now they have overstepped the mark.

They have entered your arena and have thrown down the gauntlet.

This was not a quick, snide remark made to arouse derived laughter from the audience or friends.
This was a personal attack at you and what you are doing.

So how do you proceed?

What is the best course of action?

Well first you need to find out:

What kind of heckler am I up against?

And then decide what ways are there to deal with them?

Remember that you are in a new situation, you should be able to evaluate what is going on.

The best first line of offense is defense so maybe doing nothing is the best first course.

If this is not the case then you need to work out the next course of action.

The Comic.
Have a laugh, give him some lines that are easy going he will more than likely be up for some banter.

The "Comic" does have the potential to become a bit excited, he is now part of the show and may start getting above his place.

If this happens you need to hit him a bit harder, just to let him know who is in charge.
The other problem with the "Comic" is that when other people in the audience see you having some friendly banter with him, they may be

inclined to have a go as well, and before long you have half the audience thinking they are funny.

The trend must not be set towards heckling the performer as this can lead to all kinds of problems and can invite more dangerous hecklers to take over.

The Drunk.
You need to deal with the "Drunk" in such a way that the audience dislikes the heckler and back you 100%.

You must be careful though, the "Drunk" can be like a wild animal and will get nasty if threatened, you need to knock him down in such a way that he isn't insulted.

If dealt with properly he will either just turn away and move on, laugh at you or sit down and carry on drinking.

Drinking can have a strange effect on people and when someone is drunk, there is no way of knowing what he will do.

The best idea is to use subtle and quick lines.

"I remember my first pint".

"Never drink on an empty head".

"Can we plug his chair in?"

"Go stand by the wall mate, that's plastered too".

By using a smart quick one-liner that gets a laugh you can also discover what kind of a drunk you are up against.

One common factor of any "Drunk" is that they love the sound of their own voice and that they have something to say and they want you and everyone to listen.

Sometimes the "Drunk" will retreat slightly and just shout out random comments or abuse, he will lurk near the bar or stage area and just make quick comments about you or your act.

How you deal with this is up to you, sometimes you can just ignore him or just use smart lines back, or even make a point of noticing him when he starts to head back over, something along the lines of,

"*Oooh here he comes again, more amazing words of wisdom will follow*".

"*We will be back straight after this advert from the local brewery*".

After he hears the audience laughing at what you are saying and not at what he is saying, and that they are laughing **at** him and not **with** him, he will either shut up or leave. Even so you must still be ready to hit him harder if need be.

The other option you have by this stage is to ask security to remove the heckler. If you have the audience behind you and he is just being a nuisance then get him removed.

The Hardcore.
The "Hardcore", is very similar to the school bully, he likes to show his strength, but when you hit back he doesn't like it, this however is your best choice of defence.

It is a difficult game, he needs to be struck hard every time but if you go too far he will join forces with his mates and "Group" heckle you, it's a long shot but you need to get his mates on your side, it takes some doing but it is not impossible.

He is going to be a difficult one because he is ready for you, and your lines, and this makes your job twice as hard.

He also has a large group of friends behind him, they will think his abuse is funny so you already have big laughs against you from his friends.

There are a couple of tactics here, you can get him up and try and get him on side, he will not be expecting this approach, he may be a "Hardcore" but up on stage they are in unfamiliar territory, this is usually enough to quieten them down, especially as any jeers from his mates will be aimed at him.

If this doesn't work you can now face real trouble, you have invited him in front of the audience and pretty much allowed him to do whatever he wants on your say so.

I have seen hecklers in this instance stand behind the performer and pull a Moon, or shout abuse or just be disruptive, it depends what you plan to do when you have the heckler up as to whether this is the correct course of action to take.

My favourite method is to get one of his mates up, and turn them into the focus of attention, again this can be dangerous, but the cronies of the "Hardcore" are normally not as loud, strong willed or prepared for the attention they are about to get (members of the armed forces are an exception to this rule), you can get some laughs from the audience and his mates and keep the show moving.

Afterwards you can send him back to his mates, the "Hardcore" has had his 5lbs of flesh and entertainment and it wasn't at his expense.

From experience you shouldn't get much more abuse from the "Hardcore" who will normally move on to the bar or stand at the back talking to his mates. He wasn't and still isn't interested in your show, but he has left his mark and defended his territory and can now look for his next conquest, usually the barmaid.

You must be prepared if they do carry on, you must still remain in control and be prepared to push the envelope a bit further, remember the "Hardcore" is a bully and responds best to being put in his place, you must do this without turning the audience against you.

I usually open with some lines like for the "Drunk", but you have to be ready to hit him with some harder ones like

"*He has a kind face, the kind you want to smash through the window*"

"*You remind me of a bunch of roses, there's always one prick in every bunch*"

Once you have dealt with the "Hardcore" it will put others off heckling.

The would be or failed comedian.
I try not to be too hard with this one, they can be a dangerous one if cornered but if you give him a bit of rope he will probably hang himself anyway so you might as well help him along, he likes to think he has the ability to be funny.

I usually find that if you get a laugh **with** the "Would Be", he will then shut up for the rest of the act. You can spot the "Would Be" quite quickly. They will be loud and like the attention his voice gets him.

The "Would Be" also has the potential like the "Comic" to go over the top, so be aware of how long you carry on.

If you decide to use lines you can hit with some funny but not too harsh ones like these:

"*Have you seen play school? You're going through the square window*".

"*I wouldn't let your mind wander, it's too small to go out on its own*".

He is normally happy to get a bit of attention and will want to help you have a better show, let him jump through a few hoops for you and then leave him alone.

Let him know that he has had his moment and now you have to carry on.

Give a few lines then ignore him, he will soon get the message.

This kind of heckler will almost always approach you after the show with comments like,

"*you love that interaction stuff don't you mate?*"
"*I only did it to help you*".
"I could have been a comedian".

The group heckler.
Sometimes they will be like the "Would Be", sometimes not, I have encountered groups who want nothing more than to completely ruin my show, and others who have given me the opportunity to stay in control and have a bloody good laugh as well.

If they want to ruin you, find the ringleader and treat like the "Hardcore". This is the only way you will get any control back, you need to show them who is in charge.

If they act like the "Would Be" incorporate them, use them and move on.

If you use audience members in your show, get one of these up, like I mentioned in the "Hardcore", however with the "Group" I will get one of the louder ones up, take the Mickey for 5-10 minutes and then send them back to the group with their tail between their legs.

In these cases the "Group" leader will almost always have a drink waiting for me when I leave the stage.

Unlike the "Hardcore" the loudest in a "Group" is normally the one who always gets the most stick from his mates, so by getting him up and having a laugh you have effectively become part of their little gang.

One word of warning though, know where the line is and don't cross it, be nice and have a laugh but don't push it too far or the whole group can turn nasty towards you.

The female heckler.
VERY DANGEROUS, you must proceed very carefully against this one.

You can lose your audience here so easily, the wrong line, sound of voice or gesture and they will turn on you so fast your feet will hardly touch the floor.

Of all the hecklers out there the "Female" is the one I am most afraid of.

You have to start very smoothly, they are out to ruin you, but you must stay professional at all times. In some cases lines will not work.

I have tried everything from heckle lines to simply asking them to be quiet. Sometimes though you just have to grab the bull by the horns and go for it.

The "Female" heckler will normally run along a similar route, they will be very abusive very quickly, they feel that they are untouchable and I use this to my advantage, as my show isn't blue in nature, I can push my envelope further by staying away from obscene material, and by not being offensive.

"She was nicer to me in the toilet"

"Last time you heckled me you were in the same dress"

These lines while not nasty or vindictive will hit the mark and let them know that you are not afraid to make fun at their expense, this takes their belief of being invincible away and lets me remain the dominant person.

This is not for the faint hearted though and you must be careful not to lose the audience, if you are in doubt then forget it and try something else.

I cannot express more that you have a very dangerous opponent here, they will shout abuse at you worse than you may ever hear and then turn around, smile sweetly at the manager and complain that you picked on her and insulted her.

Chapter Twenty One
If They Still Carry On Heckling

(Using the heckle lines)

So you have used a couple of lines and now the heckler has carried on. You throw some more lines at him and still he will not shut up, now you try a last few lines and it still has not worked.

The attempt to outwit him has failed and he is still throwing heckles at you.

STOP!

Analyse the situation, have you made the right choice on the lines you are using. Did you think he was drunk, and now realise he is not drunk. If you have made the right moves and applied the right techniques then now you have to look at what you are going to do now.

What is the next step?

Change the method of dealing with hecklers.
This is the most commonly used option.

You must now decide the best alternate method of dealing with this situation.

I have seen many performers who have been using heckle lines, just stop and ask the heckler to be quiet.

It's very direct and It can have 2 effects:

It works.
The heckler stops, well done! Now you have to keep the audience on side and carry on.

You have shown that you are good for a laugh and you do not mind a bit of banter, but you are not there to be messed about.

It doesn't work.
The heckler laughs and carries on. They have got to you and now they know it.

It's like the annoying kid at school who winds you up, and when you break and shout back they laugh and push harder.

If this happens you have to really evaluate your approach and make some fast manoeuvres to regain the respect of the audience.

Keep going with the same approach.
I don't like this, it is risky, you have failed to contain the problem and now it may appear that you are desperate and grasping at straws.

You will start to deal the heckle lines harder and faster, until you end up looking incompetent, outdone and unprofessional.

If they are just trying to have a laugh and not being vindictive then acknowledge the laugh and then turn away from the heckler and carry on.

Ignore any further comments and the heckler should get the idea.

Chapter Twenty Two
If They Still Carry On Heckling

(Without using the heckle lines)

So here we are again, but this time we are not using heckle lines.

Some people might like to try and deal with the situation without using heckle lines and then if they do not work to move over to the other system of using heckle lines, or vice versa.

There are methods in each that would serve either preference.

Let's have a look at the techniques that will work in this situation?

The Comic.
The "Comic" responds well to the "Laugh" approach, he feels that he has got his laugh and also been thanked for it. I will deliver the "*Cheers mate*" with a smile and a short nod so as to acknowledge him.

If he carries on, I stop what I am doing for a second, look straight at him and say, "*Hold on mate*", and then carry on.

If this technique doesn't work, I move onto the "Quiet Approach". "The Comic" will not normally want to destroy your act, so he will soon get the message and back down.

The Drunk.
You have to be careful against the "Drunk", if you treat them wrong they can turn nasty. The best approach here is to go straight for the "Quiet" and also to use the "Silent" if they persist.

Let them know they are ruining the show for everyone else.

You need to keep the audience behind you. The "Drunk" will be unpopular so use that as well.

The good thing about the drunk is that they want to be popular and funny so if you tell them they are ruining the show, it will normally have the desired effect.

Usually once dealt with the "Drunk" will not try again.

The Hardcore or Idiot.
This will not be easy. You have to keep going and not let the heckles distract you.

The "Hardcore" is fuelled by the fact that he is annoying and disrupting you. You can talk over him, completely ignore him and carry on.

When he sees you are not going to indulge him he will either intensify his assault or quieten down.

A good approach here is to use the "Silent" just long enough so he is annoying everyone then give him the "Quiet".

It's a good way of getting the message across in a strong and professional way.

The Would Be or Failed Comedian.
Follow the advice given for the "Comic". Don't be too hard, let them have their two seconds and then carry on.

They are never going to be funny but they really want to be. If you are nice to them and not too harsh you will be able to direct them to believing they have helped and will settle down.

Again if they persist follow the method above.

The Group Heckler.
Once again the method used for the "Hardcore" is relevant here, but this time aimed at the whole group or the group leader.

Use the "Silent" just long enough so they are annoying everyone then use the "Quiet".

The main differences here are that there are more than one of them and you need to deal with the situation quickly.

This method is the best way, it keeps you in charge and turns the audience away from the heckler.

The Female Heckler.
Dealing with the "Female" is never easy. You must use all the information at your disposal to continue.

The "Female" will be very abusive very quickly, the best way is to just go straight for the "Quiet".

Tell them in no certain terms that they are to quieten down.

The Child Heckler.
To stop the "Child" heckler use the same info as above in the Female, but aim it at the parents.

If they are embarrassed they will keep junior quiet.

Like the drunk, they will be unpopular with the rest of the audience, nobody likes a cocky kid, so stay in charge and tell them to be quiet and then carry on.

Chapter Twenty Three
Crossing The Line

What happens when you cross the line?
You have taken things a bit far and you upset or offend someone.

Okay, remember "*Don't Panic*", you have made a mistake, and now you have to deal with it.

Three things could happen:

- The audience will start to show their disapproval by booing, jeering, shouting etc.

- The offended person gets nasty.

- Nothing and / or the offended person walks out or sits down.

Sometimes you will get a combination of all three.
Let's look at all three scenarios

The audience turns against you.
This is a hard one, you will have a real uphill battle against you and you have to keep that stage smile on as you move onto the next part of your show.

It is not easy, some of the audience will be annoyed but most times you can regroup and continue your act until the end.

If the person has been so abusive that you had to deliver a really nasty put-down, you will probably be able to rekindle some kind of relationship with the audience.

If this is the case, a simple,

"Sorry you all had to see that"

may be enough to console the audience, maybe not.

It's a really nasty place to be in, you will really have to work the crowd to get them back on side.

If however you have just gone in too hard too quickly, then you need to look at the approach you use.

It's very easy to lose yourself and hit hard too quickly.

Your first line gets a laugh and the person heckles again and you go straight for a killer put down.

You destroy any relationship you have with the audience and have to start again with them annoyed at you.

Remember you are a professional and therefore in the eyes of the audience you should act like one.

The offended person turns nasty.
This is a tricky one, you can recover if you act properly, but you have to move carefully.

If the audience is complaining as well, you have to deal with the offended person first, once he is quiet you can recover the audience as above.

If you try to deal with the audience before you deal with the heckler then he will just carry on making a nuisance and will possibly get others to start shouting as well, so deal with him first and then move onto the audience afterwards.

If the audience hasn't changed pace, it's very possible that they didn't even hear what you said.

Here you can, with some manoeuvring, recover and carry on to finish your show.

It will depend on how you wish to deal with the situation as what to do next, ignore the person, ask him to be quiet and sit down, carry on as if nothing has happened, or speak to them off the microphone.

Here you will have to use your own intelligence to decide what the best course of action should be.

Nothing happens and / or the offended person walks out or sits down.
A couple of things may have happened here,

The audience is not responding because they didn't hear what was said.

They didn't understand what was said.

They thought it was all part of the banter or didn't find it offensive.

If this is the case then carry on, the heckler will not like you, but the audience will be none the wiser. If the heckler has sat down or left the room then the situation has dissolved.

Just be aware of what you did and try not to cross the line again.

If you do cross the line then you need to act quickly and professionally.

Keep your cool and keep the show moving forward.

Any action you take will have to be decided quickly and without the pace of the show being slowed.

It's a horrible feeling when you lose the audience, but it happens to the best of us, you just have to keep going and learn from what has happened.

Chapter Twenty Four
Losing To The Heckler

The worst nightmare of any performer is to lose to the heckler.

They say,

"The man with the microphone, never loses"

If only this were true.

So why does it happen?

It happens because:

- The performer is inexperienced and doesn't see it coming.

- The performer is too arrogant to see it coming.

- The heckler is a professional.

- All or some of the above.

The inexperienced performer.
Classic hallmarks of an inexperienced performer are pushing the heckler too far or by using the wrong approach.

What will happen here is that the heckler swipes your feet out from under you, you're now on a slippery slope and nothing will stop you sliding to the bottom.

The arrogant performer.
I have seen many arrogant performers take a fall, and unfortunately most of the time they have deserved it.

The heckler will use the audience against you, here is an example.

Singing the blues.
I was watching a singer on stage and in between his songs he was telling some mild jokes.

A lot of his humour was based around taking the mickey out of people in the audience.

This particular performer had very quickly alienated himself from the room.

He was trying to poke fun at a table with two couples on, one of the men was at the bar getting drinks and at the table was the other man and the two women.

He kept making swipes at the man at the table and before too long the man at the bar decided enough was enough and started heckling.

The singer decided that he was much better than the heckler and so tried to hit him with some completely random lines and failed over and over again.

After a few failed attempts at fighting the heckler the performer says,

"*You shouldn't drink on an empty head*".

Not a bad line but obviously should be used against a drunken heckler not as a random line.

The heckler came back with,

"*You shouldn't sing with a crap voice*".

This visibly shook the singer as it got a very big laugh from the audience and he hesitated for a fraction of a second before he unwisely decided to hit back with a similar line.

"*I wish you were a statue and I was a pigeon*"

Not a great line, and one I have never used because it opens yourself up to the reply that this act got.

The heckler replied,

"*That is because you are full of shit*".

Game over, the whole audience erupted with laughter and started shouting at the singer to get off.

The audience laughed **AT** the performer and **WITH** the heckler, because he hadn't made a rapport with the audience, when he tried to rally them to his aid, he couldn't.

In this instance if the performer hadn't been so full of himself he wouldn't have been put in the situation in the first case.

I watched the heckler get more annoyed because the singer was trying to make his friend look stupid and in the end the audience rallied behind the heckler, he was their spokesman and they stood behind him.

When the performer left the stage it was met with loud cheers and clapping.

Unfortunately the applause was not for him.

The professional heckler.
The professional heckler will unleash either a pre-planned heckle that he has used before and knows will kill, or he will just get lucky and say the right thing at the right time.

When it happens, that heckle will keep you awake for a very long time.

Can I stop this from happening to me?

Yes you can, and it's very simple, show respect for your audience and build a rapport with them. The story above illustrates this.

The heckler only started because of the way the performer was acting towards his group, he created a situation that could have been avoided.

Remember in most cases,
Prevention is better than a Cure

If you are going to start a fire, make sure you have the necessary means to control it and extinguish it.

Chapter Twenty Five
The Three Strike Rule

This is not for everyone. The plan will involve you setting up the heckler for a big fall and then taking his legs out from under him, getting you the big laugh and finishing the heckler at the same time.

The three strike rule is,

You use a heckle line that gets a laugh.
Strike 1

You use a second heckle line that gets a bigger laugh.
Strike 2

You use a killer heckle line and take out the heckler.
Strike 3

I have done this a few times, but you really have to know the system. It must all be exact, this is a precision manoeuvre that requires exact timing.

The set up and the audience must be perfectly aligned, and if the audience is not **100%** behind you then forget it.

I am going to describe a heckler that I used this method on. It wasn't particularly subtle and it was a rough crowd in a rough English bar in the middle of Salou, a holiday resort in Spain.

I had done my show in the bar many times and knew I could get away with this, so I went for it.

The three strike rule in action

It was approximately 11.40pm, I had been on stage for around 40 minutes and a drunk guy had been heckling me for most of my show.
I had used some lines on him and he was responding each time with abuse, in a few short minutes he had made a complete fool of himself and now I wanted him to shut up so I could finish the show.

He quieted down for a few minutes and as I was thanking the bar staff and the DJ host, the heckler started again to throw some offensive abuse.

The bouncers and bar manager were standing directly behind the heckler and were waiting for a nod from me to say that they could get rid of him.

I must point out here that this venue had the best staff you could ever want.

The doormen were the most professional I have ever met and would never make a move without the proper go-ahead. They understood the need of the performer to control the room.

All I would need to do is nod my head at the head bouncer and he would remove the offender straight away.

It was right at the end of my show and I needed to finish in the proper way. I decided (rightly or wrongly) to set up the heckler and use it to my advantage, to get a big laugh and then as the audience were laughing, finish him off with a bigger laugh and then close the show.

The heckler was very abusive, but without reason, I hadn't picked on him, belittled or abused him in any way shape or form, he was quite drunk but not incoherent, suddenly and without reason he stood up and walked to the edge of the performance area (a small raised section) and shouted at me,

"*F#ck off the stage, give me the mic*".

(Yeah like that would ever happen).

He then told me,

"*You are f#cking crap and ugly*".

(He may be drunk, but at least his eyesight was good).

I hit him with a mildly funny line,

"*I thought alcoholic's were supposed to be anonymous?*" **(Strike 1)**.

This got the desired laugh but he instantly hit back with,

"*You're fat*".

I knew I had to finish this quickly, so I moved into attack positions.

The next two lines would be delivered hard and fast, no time for the heckler to say another word.

I turned my body to look at the heckler, but spoke to the room as a whole,

"*I really wish we were better strangers*".
(Strike 2)

The laughter was loud, so I immediately followed up with,

"*Honestly, how many times do I have to flush, before you will go away?*"
(Strike 3)

The response was amazing, the audience went crazy and as they applauded I said over the laughing and clapping,

"*Thank you and Goodnight*".

As I left the stage, most of the audience were on their feet, clapping and cheering and loving this impromptu and unique ending for my show.

The heckler was lost in a sea of people and realised that he was defeated.

As I walked off stage, the last thing I saw was him slumped back in his seat, alone and staring at his beer.

I set him up and I took him down and the whole exchange from start to finish was less than 30 seconds.

The line was delivered, a pause to let the punchline sink in, laugh and then the next line was delivered.

No time was given to the heckler to try and find his feet before he could respond, I was already starting my next line.

It wasn't how I wanted to end the show, I could have just had the bouncers drag him from the room, but that would have killed the atmosphere; I finished the show with the respect of the audience.

Wayne's Note:
Some people reading this may disagree with my actions and might have sought a better way to deal with him.

It's not easy but you have to make a decision instantly and you may later decide this course of action was right or wrong.

I will never forget that night, I learned a lot from the experience and to this day feel I took the right course of action.

On that night, I felt that the audience was on my side and he had overstepped the mark, if there had been one tiny piece of uncertainty, it would never have happened.

Chapter Twenty Six
Things You Can Use Against The Heckler

Put down lines.
Put down's can be the performer's best friend or worst enemy.

I have covered put down lines in other chapters, but they do have a place here too.

Microphone.
It's an old adage that says,
"The Man with the Microphone always wins".
It is not strictly true but it does make a good point, that the man with the microphone does control the room.

You have the ability to talk over the heckler and maintain control.

The heckler will try and say something and you have the ability to just cut him off, it is rude but it's effective. Check out George Carlin, he just ignores people who shout out.

Lights.
Using the house lights as a weapon against the heckler can be very effective.

In some venues you may be lucky enough to have a single spotlight, this is rare but it does happen.

The spotlight operator can be instructed to shine the light directly onto the heckler so that everyone can see them.

Now when you use a line on them or ask them to be quiet, it is much more powerful because the whole audience will be looking at them.

The pressure of trying to heckle, keep ahead of the performer and be under the spotlight, is normally enough to quell any further interruptions.

Tricks.

There are literally thousands of effects on the market that are ideal for using against a heckler.

Personally I do not like using them, it may well suit your style and persona but I think they are a bad idea, mainly because you are now dedicating a portion of your show to defeating a heckler.

You have moved from having a bit of a laugh to a change in the show.

Allowing a disruptive heckler to have a major input in the show can be a recipe for disaster, you are basically giving them "Carte Blanche".

You need to be able to maintain the highest levels of control.

If this is the kind of performance you desire it can work wonders for you, I know many comedians whose acts are solely devised for getting people to heckle and then dealing with them.

Audience.

As I have put throughout the book your greatest weapon against the heckler is the audience.

You can use the audience but only after you have built their respect.

In the next chapter we will look at how we utilise the audience as an asset.

Chapter Twenty Seven
Using The Audience

Many times in this book you will hear me refer to the fact that you need to use the audience. So how do you do this?

How do you make the audience like you?

How do you make them dislike the heckler?

How can you make them go in the direction that you want them to?

The audience is a funny thing, they are all individuals but they move and react as one.

This is not unlike a flock of birds flying in their formations, they are all capable of independent flight manoeuvres, but they stay in configuration because they are led by a single bird that takes them and directs them.

You must learn how to lead!

For example we will look at my cabaret show here.

Wayne Goodman Cabaret Show

My show is approx one hour long and features:

Lots of jokes about myself and my life.

Lots of jokes about the audience.

Lots of laughter.

Audience participation.

Some emotional contact.

Honesty among deceit.

Improvisation and the zany moments.

Obvious performer enjoyment.

Respect.

Now let's take these and break them down and look at the individual elements

Lots of jokes about myself and my life.
I am a 6ft, slightly (ahem) overweight, funny faced fool.

Often described as Harry Potter on steroids and I take great care to make sure that I am the target of a lot of my own jokes.

I take the mickey out of my life, job, girlfriend, friends, family and anything else that is connected to me.

Lots of jokes about the audience.
I make a lot of jokes about the people in the audience, not in a harsh, vindictive or spiteful way, more of a friendly poke at where they are from and what they do for a living.

Lots of laughter.
From the audience but also from me, I will feign laughter if I need to, but most of the time I will laugh naturally, even at my own jokes.

The reason for this is simply that I find them funny, if I don't think my jokes are funny, then why should the audience?

Just because I have heard them thousands of times is irrelevant, I only tell jokes that I find funny.

I do not just spend the whole show laughing at my own jokes, but a lot of my one-liners are aimed to look like ad libs, which means a giggle or chuckle is not out of place.

If a person assisting me or in the audience makes a funny remark or comment I will laugh at it, and not be afraid to compliment the person for their remark.

Audience participation.
Nearly every trick I perform involves at least one member of the audience, even if it is just to shuffle a pack of cards or lend me their shirt, (to use in the effect).

I believe that involving people from the audience takes the show to them and makes them more emotionally involved.

Some emotional contact.
The tricks, jokes and stories that I tell are not just placed in the show for a laugh, they are placed to get maximum use for me as a performer.

Some of the jokes are used as basic misdirection whilst others make an emotional contact with the audience as a whole.

I want to bond with the audience and make them feel comfortable and relaxed in my presence, and then they will allow me to do what I do.

Honesty among deceit.
My show is a show of lies,

I do not hate my girlfriend.

I cannot really perform magic.

The small furry animal in the box isn't really alive.

I lie to the audience so that I can try and be honest with the audience.

I want them to like me and I want them to enjoy what I have to show them.

I want them to remember **ME**, not what I did, or what I told them, it's all about **ME**.

Improvisation and the zany moments.
As much as my show is organised, I cannot help that a part of me loves the unpredictable. If I see a situation occurring in the room I will use the opportunity and make the most of it.

Many of the comments I get regarding my show are based on the fact that people think I make it up as I go along.

People like to see things happen off the cuff and out of the blue, it makes them think the show is fresh and a one off special event just for them.

Obvious performer enjoyment.
I love magic, I love performing and I love the reaction that I get from an audience.

The audience enjoys my show and can see that I am enjoying it as well.

I always believe that the audience feeds off the energy of the performer.

Respect.
For me respect is the most important part when using an audience. I respect them as a group and as individuals.

Even though I take the mickey and have a laugh with the volunteers or the audience, I do so with a smile and always remember that they are the clients and that they are to be made the real stars of the show.

Breaking down the show.
So there we have it, the main parts of my show laid bare, now let's have a look at how I use these elements to organise and lead the audience exactly where I wish to take them.

Remember this is my method, it may not work for you or your show, but you can take this as a model and apply it to your own show.

Lots of jokes about myself and my life.
This is important for building a bond with the audience, by making fun of yourself you will be able to show that you are good for a laugh and do not mind the people laughing at your expense.

Lots of jokes about the audience.
Once I have had a good laugh at myself, I start to involve the audience in the same way.

You have to make sure you don't do this the wrong way or you can alienate yourself. By making fun of myself and then slowly having a laugh at the audience it makes them feel like they are part of the show.

Lots of laughter.
When you have the audience laughing at what you are saying you have created a bond with them, they like you, and they are listening to what you have to say, I use comedy to keep their attention and strengthen the bond.

Audience participation.
When you choose a member of the audience to help. You are creating a very strong bond with that person, you have asked for their trust and they have (maybe not so willingly) given it.

You must be very careful how you treat this person, one wrong move and you won't be getting anyone else up and that can destroy your act, it would destroy mine.

Some emotional contact.
Once you have made an emotional impact on the audience you can then use that to maximise applause and guide the audience where you want to go.

David Copperfield is a master at creating emotional bonds with the audience. His shows are full of stories about himself and his family.

The audience reacts because of the connection created through the bond he has established.

Honesty among deceit.
The audience knows the truth about my show but by supporting their desire to suspend their disbelief I am able to create a bond.

The audience needs to believe you, so when the time comes and you need their support you can lead them in the direction you need them to go.

Improvisation and the zany moments.
I use a lot of improvisation in my act so when a heckler begins to heckle, I have the parameters to move left and right without deviating off course.

The audience is aware that I don't follow a straight line and therefore I won't lose them if I do stray off course a little.

Obvious performer enjoyment.
Once the audience is on-board with you, and they are in your zone, they will not want to be taken out of it. Any heckler will not only be facing you but the rest of the audience.

Respect.
Respect the audience, and they will respect you. It really is that simple. This is the first thing you need to build a connection with the audience.

Once you have their respect and made a connection with the audience, you have them in your zone, you are ready to use them to your advantage.

This can be for any reason, to get a reaction for an effect, to deal with a heckler, to misdirect or simply to build that emotional hook for the next routine.

Once you achieve this, you will find it easier to choose volunteers, get them on stage and the audience will be in a better position to enjoy what you are doing.

This is no different to what a fiction writer does to keep you reading, they create hooks that draw you in and keep you turning pages.

You need to learn to do this with your audience so that they keep watching, assisting and, to a certain extent not heckling.

Chapter Twenty Eight
The Close-Up Magician

A lot of people who perform close-up magic use comedy in their shows, and this can lead to some heckling.

"Can you do the trick that Dynamo did?"

"Do it again"

"It's in the other hand"

The main and most important difference between working on a stage and being heckled, and working in a close up show is that now you are in the personal space of the audience.

Using the wrong kind of response could mean that you talk yourself into a lot of trouble.

If you are not the kind of performer who can interact in this manner, then your best bet will be to brush off any heckles, have a laugh and then carry on.

We have to remember we are not the centre of the universe in this situation.

The people are there to enjoy a meal, wedding or whatever and now you are there with your cards and sponge balls and trying to impress them with some miracles.

The bad news.
The bad news is that the spectators don't need you, they didn't wake up that morning and think that if they don't see any close up magic today they will miss out or suffer.

On the other hand, you do need them and without them watching you, there is no cheque at the end of the night.

If they complain to the manager about you, then you are the loser, you can hit them with the funniest put down, but he will be the one laughing at the end.

The good news.
When you work close-up, the spectators want to feel that they can have a laugh with you, if you can bring them into your performance, then you can manipulate any heckles into being a positive for the show.

Most of the time, people will heckle in a fun way.

You will get a few idiots who may be disruptive, but just as you are in their personal space, they are outside of your performance control.

What I mean by this, is that when you are on stage, you are under the restrictions of the performance area.

When you are working close up, if you get someone who is causing a problem or just being rude, you can simply walk away and carry on at another table.

If the heckle is a fun poke at you, or what you are doing, then embrace it.

I have a number of lines that are aimed at me. I use them when I need people to warm to my humour, most are aimed at the fact that I am a large man, so a quick line like,

"I love doing sit ups, as I get to lie down every few seconds."

"I put my belt on with a boomerang."

will normally put the spectators on my side and show them that I am not afraid to have a laugh at my expense.

I like to put people around the table at ease, a simple line, like those above, let's the spectators know that you are in charge but without being nasty. This is always a good way to quell any rebellious intentions.

Back in the day, the comedy clubs, working men's clubs and the cabaret venues were the hecklers hunting ground. Today the close up worker must also endure wisecracks and jokes aimed at them.

Chapter Twenty Nine
In Conclusion

The world of entertainment is a diverse and complicated one.

What you have in this book are my thoughts, concepts and ideas on the subject of heckling.

While these worked for me, it would be foolish to assume that they would work for every situation.

As a performer, you need to look at your show, personality and the best way to respond to any and every disruption that fits the style of your performance.

To finish the book I thought I would share two stories.

The first story happened to me and is a show I think about often. I learnt a lot from this performance.

The Workers.
The holiday resort of Salou in Spain is a summer resort, during the off months a number of workers keep the British community alive with Christmas, Easter and other winter time parties and celebrations.

One is the workers' start of season party, I volunteered to perform for the workers after their Salou bars football match.

The time came for me to start, I went on stage the whole audience had been drinking all day, and the last thing they want to see is some sober bloke trying to be funny with some ropes and a Rocky Raccoon.

To say I was heckled would be an understatement.

I was bombarded with heckle after heckle, it was the longest 40 minutes of my life.

All I could see was my mate standing at the side of the stage, well corner of the bar left untouched by bottles etc for me to stand in, smiling and giving me the thumbs up sign (what show was he watching).

I stood my ground, got the main ringleader up, dealt him a few lines, some harsh, some not so harsh and made sure that at the end it was me that got the final laugh of the show.

The Last story in the book is one that did not happen to me but instead happened to a performer who worked for me.

He failed because he did not plan or prepare.

Act your Age.
(Getting it wrong)
A young magician, (who at the time was in his late teens) wanted to try out some new material.

He hadn't been performing for very long but managed to get himself a spot in a family bar, the bar is normally a good place to perform and I had done my show there many times and didn't think he would get any trouble.

The magician started off well, but unfortunately he didn't really connect too well with the audience and he started to flounder.

About half way through the show a drunken woman started heckling him, telling him to act his age etc.

He decided (wrongly) that he needed to hit back hard and fast and decided to say;

"Come on love, I don't come to the brothel and disturb you while you're working "

Her husband stood up, started shouting and mayhem erupted everywhere. The show was stopped and the performer removed before he had to face the wrath of the audience and the woman's husband.

He should have thought better and evaluated the audience before choosing the line that he did.

His age was a major factor, he was too young and too cheeky, add a few years and a more mature persona, and he may have stood a better chance but he came over as a petulant upstart who thought he knew better.

In a different environment you may get away with a line like that, but in that type of venue, a more subtle approach was needed.

Notes:

Wayne Goodman

Books by Wayne Goodman:
The Comedy Magicians Joke Book vol 1.
The Comedy Magicians Joke Book vol 2.
The Comedy Magicians Joke Book vol 3.
The Complete Comedy Magicians Joke Book.
The Definitive Guide to Restaurant Magic re-released in 2019 as
The Expert at the Restaurant Table.
Plan, Prepare, Perform - re-released in 2020 as Parabellum
Go Compere.
Maxims Primer

Booklets by Wayne Goodman:
The Jedi Principle.
The Lean.
The Restaurant Course.

Tricks by Wayne Goodman:
Lord of the Bling.
Look Sharp.
Prism.
Clone.
Marked.
Sam the bell hog.
Asbo.
Time Traveller.
Royal Brainwave.
WG Comedy Prediction.
421 Card.

By Wayne and Charlee Goodman:
Cook with Charlee.
Amazing jokes for 8 - 10 year olds.

www.ingramcontent.com/pod-product-compliance
Lightning Source LLC
Chambersburg PA
CBHW070741230426
43669CB00014B/2530